Setting The Stage: 7 Customer Retention Tactics

For the Restaurateur

By Shirley Coello

DEDICATION

I find it honest, respectful, and justified, somewhat even poetic, to dedicate my first book to W&L Catering. As I sit and ponder the reasons (there are many), as tears come to my eyes, I remember my first boss, my first responsibility as an employee, and my first payday for a job well done; I remember how happy I was just to be assisting someone I admired so much, so I was so surprised when she reached out and gave me three whole dollars for the work that we did together; some may think that three dollars wasn't enough, but for me it was too much, I told her I didn't need it, and she told me she knows that, and then handed it to me anyway.

My mother and father's catering business was my first stab at employment, and truly the best job I ever had. I loved assisting my mother in the hot tiny kitchen she catered from. I loved listening to her dreams of one day opening a restaurant where we could all work as a family (it never came to be). I loved the cooking lessons and the reminders she kept giving me to always think of everyone as a whole, and to never just think of yourself, or just one individual person's likes and/or dislikes. I remember the lessons about temperature checks, and timeliness as it pertains to food and delivery. I remember her lessons on presentation, as it pertains to food and those providing the service. I remember the rushed showers and changes of clothes, the smell of her perfume as she raced out the door to get to her clients. I remember the smell of fried somethings in the air, first in the house, then in the car as we journeyed to our destination.

We brought table cloths, napkins, plates, silverware or plasticware, racks, sternos, 10lb or 5lb pans, hot water, and huge Costco coolers full of food, and somehow she never forgot the little details like serving spoons, toothpicks, butter, salad dressings, etc. My mother was impressive, brilliant, and ready every time. She never missed a beat and even when she was tired no one knew it because her smile lit up the room each time. After days of cooking and preparing she would stand behind the food and serve and serve and serve, replace the pans and serve some more, all the while with a smile and quick wit. Everyone loved her, word of mouth spread, and she was the caterer to hire in our circles. Yup, my mother taught me more than this page can hold, and so I dedicate this book to W&L Catering, her business, my first job, and her baby; she did well, as well as she could, and built her business as high as it could go, and to this day if you ask anyone who is the best caterer in Brentwood NY, they will tell you, Lynne Cabell, my mother, owner of W&L Catering.

INTRODUCTION

Today customers are now being listened to, watched, counted as equals, in this rat race we call business. We're all enthralled with the brick and mortar store closings, mainly due to lack of customer visits to stores, and more customers choosing to do most or all of their shopping online to avoid...what?

68% of customers who never return to an establishment feel unappreciated, according to a study conducted by Marketing Strategist, Dan Kennedy, about why clients leave their vendors. If we are to really evaluate whether or not this statistic, amongst a plethora of others, that state very similar data, is something to take seriously, and not as lightly as we've been doing in the service industry, we would then have to reevaluate which traditional business practices must be overturned, added to, or supplemented for a more customer friendly approach, that will serve to usher in the patrons we have been losing in the past 10 years.

The current economic and health conditions of the United States, and around the world, has been blamed for the decline in restaurant patronage, but what if I were to show you that you can get those customers back, and then some? What if I were to give you the tools you need to increase your potential customers, and increase your customer retention, which in turn, increases your profits?

Let us look at 7 steps that can be taken to increase customer retention in your restaurant.

1. **Data Analysis** – It is extremely important to collect data on your customer satisfaction, with not only, food quality, but service, ambiance, and timing. Customer surveys are ideal for capturing the mindset of your visitors in real time.

2. **Staff Training** – It's amazing what a little more staff training can do for your bottom line. Incorporate more webinars (computer trainings), seminars, and individualized testing to ensure a complete understanding of your corporate structure and expectations of your employees.

3. **Statistics** – This can go along with your data analysis; there should be a monthly review of your restaurant statistics compared to the restaurant industry as a whole, and there should be special emphasis on customer retention statistics. There are many data software companies that provide precise software to help keep track of statistics, to aid restaurants in their quest to stay up to date with their current customer data reporting.

4. **Modern Updates** – Keep up to date with the latest technology and food crazes; this ensures the customer that you care about their wants and needs, as well as your own.

5. **Employee Retention** – Employee retention and customer retention go hand in hand; customers notice when there is consistent employee turnover and will begin to sense tension in the air amongst staff. It also indicates a distance between the owner and the restaurant; whether true or not, restaurant frequenters will begin to feel uncomfortable.

6. **Customer Appreciation** – Even 5-star restaurants need to have a day of giveaways, or individualized perks for consistent patrons. This allows the customer to feel appreciated, and to develop a sense of trust and relationship with the restaurant owner, creating a desire to continue to dine in your establishment.

7. **Listen** – The best and most important step to customer retention is the last step, because I want it to really sink into your memory. You must listen to your customers, period. Your customers hold the key to your success as restaurateurs; they are the only way to understanding your profit margins or lack thereof. Without listening to your customers, you will lose your restaurant within the first year, or if you are like the seventy percent that make it past the first year, you will close within three to five years; your customers will make or break you and your dream. Listen to your customers.

CHAPTER 1: DATA ANALYSIS

Collecting data is a crucial step in building all businesses, but for one reason or another, restaurant owners sometimes skip this step when evaluating their own establishment. Data analysis is designed to prepare a business for past, present, and future patronage; it gives a detailed picture of the who, what, when, where, why, and how of the restaurateur's patrons, so there can be a balanced relationship that profits everyone.

Data analysis can be achieved in many different ways. Within the last few decades, the internet has played a huge role in data analysis; restaurateurs are now able to conduct online surveys through email marketing, and many social media platforms, in order to get an assessment of their patron's mindset as they enjoy their cuisine. Restaurateurs have been known to give freebies, and/or discounts to anyone that completes their surveys, and/or writes a review for their restaurant and their service. Data analysis information can also be taken from dining surveys taken while having the experience; it makes for an honest and straight forward review, however, this way can also annoy patrons, so it's best to evaluate the kind of image your restaurant portrays, and decide from there.

Another effective way to gather data is to obtain phone numbers and/or email addresses from patrons, in order to contact them over the phone, greeting the past patron first, then getting permission to ask a few questions about their dining experience. This may not be the most popular way of gathering data, however it is one way that does get the job done; this can be outsourced to customer service agencies.

Once data is gathered, the analysis of the data begins. There are professional data analysists that are specifically licensed to analyze data; they can give you proper guidance as to how you can apply that data, creating the perfect restaurant atmosphere for your particular patrons. If you are comfortable gathering the data yourself, you can also take a look at the responses to the questions rendered, and come up with solutions to enhance your patron's experiences. This approach of data analysis will catapult your business into the next level of stars.

Questions?

Many restaurateurs get stuck when it comes to the matter of which questions to ask on a survey meant to collect data for analysis. This can be a very complicated answer because each business has its own customer focus, therefore seeking different answers to different questions, however, coming up with the right questions to ask is not impossible. Restaurateurs can analyze other restaurants who have a similar focused demographic, observe what they might find wrong with their competition and then make sure to offer the opposite of what their competition may be doing wrong; they can then create questions based on this particular difference to see if the patrons actually appreciate the difference, without having to advise the patrons of their attempt to be different from the competition, the patrons will never know, and you've collected your data.

Another way to determine the best questions to ask to get the best results, is to hire a professional data analyst specifically with a background in restaurant industry data. Data analysists can show you the best course of action when preparing questions and creating solutions to the issues that may come up. Hiring a professional in this field will surely increase restaurant profits, and in turn will have a very high return on investment.

Evaluating your patrons is a great way to come up with questions to ask on your surveys. Watching patron behaviors, attitudes, comfort levels, and mindsets, can help bolster questions that can lead to a highly informative survey that will help you in your task to create the perfect dining atmosphere for your guests.

CHAPTER 2: STAFF TRAINING

How To Train Your Restaurant Staff

Expectations

Every restaurateur has expectations that they have for all employees that work for them. They have dedicated rules and guidelines specific to their brand, and they are adamant about everyone adhering to those guidelines. It is important then for the restaurateur to make these expectations known from the very first day of hiring each and every employee. Letting your staff know how you feel about your employees, your business, and your patrons from the very beginning is the way to ensure they will respect your expectations for how your establishment is to be run.

Customer Service Basics

The art of customer service seems pretty basic, simplistic even, but don't let the minimum wage fool you, customer service is an extremely difficult task and takes years of mastering. It is important to consistently train your staff in the proper ways of the professional customer service representative in order to gain the trust of your patrons. Nowadays, if a patron has a bad customer service experience with anyone working within your facility, that bad experience travels faster than ever before, with the advent of the internet. Google reviews and the like can make or break a business with only one review; customer service training is essential now more than ever before.

Start with the basics of customer service, then continue from there to your own expectations of the staff, and your specific branding (like the greeting that all staff must give to every patron entering and/or leaving the restaurant). Training your staff with these essential professional values is an indispensable asset that must not be forgotten, no matter the industry, but especially for restaurateurs.

Ambiance

What does ambiance have to do with training? Ambiance is a major part of your staff training, as the atmosphere of your restaurant can cause potential customers to go elsewhere if your establishment is not up to the cleanly standards of most hungry potential customers. Staff must have a set schedule as to how and when to clean the establishment. Depending on the type of restaurant, staff must learn where to put certain items, when to put certain items out, and where and when to clean the restaurant as a whole. Restaurant patrons notice everything, including dusty ceilings, so it is important to address any and all areas that may become filthy throughout the day, including the bathrooms. All staff must be designated an area to clean and maintain, and then they must be given a schedule to ensure their area has not been contaminated in anyway throughout the day. Organizing a cleaning schedule and ensuring staff adhere to that schedule will allow for an ambiance that is sure to attract more restaurant goers.

Financial Training?

I know it's odd to see the title of "Financial Training?" but knowing how the restaurant gains profit, knowing how to count money, and knowing the importance of the restaurant's financial standing as it pertains to everyone, can really help put the financial aspect of the business in perspective for all employees at every pay scale. Having a monthly meeting, involving all staff, to discuss the financial expectations of the restaurant is a great way to include everyone in on how well the restaurant is doing and how the restaurant can do better. It also holds everyone in the restaurant accountable for their actions because it will show needs for improvement in some areas and give accolades where needed in other areas. Financial training can also help with those that are not so savvy on the cash register; they eventually will learn to work the register like their coworkers, becoming more well-rounded, which creates a work atmosphere of can-do employees willing to help each other out with any and all tasks within their expertise.

Food Preparation

Why would a host/hostess, omnibus, waitress need to learn food preparation? It is simple, they cannot appreciate the time and dedication it takes to cook and prepare food unless they have experienced the entire process of doing so.

An anecdote: when I worked for a convent as a salad prep, they had us prepare cold foods and the dining areas for the nuns. We would also occasionally prepare for retreats and parties for five hundred people or less. During my down time I would stay with the chefs preparing the hot foods, and learn about their techniques, which gave me much better insight into their everyday tasks, and it helped me to appreciate their job as a whole, which ultimately made me the most efficient worker there, and it helped me to enjoy my job more, as I learned new things that I never anticipated learning.

Encouraging employees to learn new tasks, can keep their job from feeling stale, and keep them from feeling stagnant. It also works as an extra pair of eyes when sending out the food to the patrons, in order to catch any mistakes or mishaps that may occur due to common error. A well-rounded, appreciated, encouraged employee is a happy, consistent, loyal employee.

Laws

Every company, including restaurants, must have bylaws that every employer and employee must abide by; these rules must be addressed from the moment a potential employee agrees to work for the company. A contract with the company rules and regulations must be signed and agreed upon, after ensuring everyone's understanding of these rules; if this act is not performed from the very beginning of employment it can mean disaster for all parties involved. Rules are rules and everyone has laws that must be adhered to, so this is a must if you want to avoid conflict of any kind.

CHAPTER 3: STATISTICS

Why We Need Them

Numbers, Uhhh!

Statistics, if you've ever taken this math class in high school or college, you know how extremely detailed and intricate statistics can be. Statistics consist of very complicated math sequences that allow us to explore options. Options can be important when trying to understand our customers, our client base, and our overall focus for marketing and campaigns; although statistical data can be quite boring for most of us, there are professionals in the world that love this stuff, that live and breathe it every day. These professionals love to look at data and compile numbers, compare, workout ratios of groups of restaurant goers, and come up with a specific algorithm to gain the most customers that love the whole theme of your restaurant, then come up with numbers to show who is more likely to come back to your restaurant by statistical analysis, who is more likely to dislike certain particulars about your restaurant, which age group you must focus on, which themes would best suit your restaurant and most importantly, which foods are best served to your potential patrons, even before one diner sets foot in your restaurant. Hiring a statistician may cost quite a bit up front, but you get your money's worth in the end. Statistics not only help increase sales through marketing to the right demographic, but it also decreases expenses, as restaurateurs spend considerably less on marketing, ambiance, and food varieties when they use statistics to pinpoint a specific concentration, saving exponential amounts of startup cash by reducing time, money, and resources potentially wasted on uninterested patrons, disliked foods, and unnecessary décor.

Customer Retention And Statistics

Simply put, if you get ahead of the statistics of your specific restaurant theme and genre before your doors even open to the public, you will conquer your market, period. Statistics not only tell you who you should market to, but how and why you should market to your audience. Statistics show you what went wrong with other restaurants within your specialty, so that you don't make the same mistakes; statistics show you exactly what your audience is looking for, where they want it and how they want it. Statistics tell the answers to everything you need to know before you even open your restaurant, and if you follow the numbers, your patrons will continue to come back time and time again because you are giving them exactly what they want.

- ❖ Who will be interested in your restaurant?

- ❖ What will your patrons be interested in the most?

- ❖ When will the most diners decide to come into the restaurant and what time will the restaurant have the least amount of diners?

- ❖ Where is the best location for your restaurant, for those most likely to frequent your restaurant?

- ❖ Why will your diners love your restaurant the most?

- ❖ How can you give your diners exactly what they're looking for and, most importantly, how can you keep them happy?

Only statistics can give you the inside scoop on the who, what, when, where, why, how, before one patron steps through your doors, and will continue to give you this most important data throughout the life of your business. Whether you decide to utilize software or hire professionals, statistics will carry your business into notoriety within your genre, if you just pay attention to the numbers.

CHAPTER 4: MODERN UPDATES

Technology

You Can Do This

Within the last two decades keeping up with technology has been an uphill battle for most, especially those of us that grew up when the internet wasn't even a word used in common practice, so hearing the words, "keep up to date with the latest..." can be overwhelming and somewhat intimidating, however, keeping up with the latest technology doesn't have to be that complicated, especially for restaurant owners, here's why:

I.T. Department

You can always outsource any of your Information Technology issues and call it an IT department. Pay someone that loves keeping up with all of the latest technology to update you on the latest trends in restaurant software, and what restaurant patrons are looking for within your specific restaurant culture, as far as the Wi-Fi access, ease of ordering, whether online or dining in, and ease of payments. You can even keep up to date with the latest survey technology that may help in encouraging your patrons to offer up their thoughts about your establishment. You can outsource this job to anyone and work out a payment plan that is best for both of you, whether monthly or every few months, or even on a per diem basis; the payments can be up to you and your specialist, but will be worth it when your patrons admire your tech savvy restaurant filled with all of the latest gadgets and gizmos to keep them interested while they dine.

Modernize Your Food Offerings

Food crazes can be the best and worst ideas for restaurants to try and duplicate or dominate in the restaurant world of keeping up with the Jones'. People are finicky, and one day they are in love with a certain type of food and the next day loathe it (like me and anchovies). Restaurateurs have a lot on their plate when it comes to pleasing their patrons, and choosing which meals to offer is no different, no matter the genre chosen within the industry.

❖ Fast-food – Fast-food can be a pretty simple genre to partake in as a restaurateur; hamburgers, french fries, sodas are the basics, then you add your chicken options and fish options, and you have yourself a fast-food restaurant; so where do the crazes come in? Fast-food has a lot of competition, and competitions cause crazes within the industry. As marketing teams create themes that ensure their restaurant stands out, other restaurants within the fast-food genre have to keep up. Due to competition, the simple basics of fast-food can become outrageously complicated, and keeping up with modern food crazes or trends can become a full-time job alone. Marketing teams must always follow competition and decide what new thing they might come out with for a specific season, and make sure to offer something similar, while staying one step ahead of the competition, with additional offerings and/or better flavor; and it wouldn't hurt to come up with their own new trend, like pumpkin spice flavored options for the fall.

❖ Fine Dining – Of course, fast-food restaurants aren't the only restaurant genres that face competition within their genres, all restaurants do, so all restaurants must be diligent in staying up to date with their patrons and what they expect from their dining experience. For instance, there are a lot of restaurants now that offer a menu that will show wine suggestions paired with a specific meal, other restaurants soon followed suit as this option became a welcome addition to the fine dining experience. Other restaurants still feel their patrons would like it better if the waiter/waitress was to offer his/her recommendations, and would rather not list wine suggestions on their menus for their patrons; what a restaurant offers widely has to do more with what their regular patrons are showing interest in, and less about looking at the general public's opinion, which is why statistical analysis for your regular patrons is so important when modernizing and updating your restaurant as a whole.

❖ Bar & Grill, Lounges – These types of restaurants are known to offer great nightlife options, which can be a hotbed for competition, so modernizing and updates are essential for longevity. Bars that are known to offer a plethora of drinks and discounts are usually the bars most frequented by their customer demographic, so it is important to stay on top of the latest alcohol trends and weekday offerings to keep patrons coming in. The latest trend for bars and lounges in 2020 has been the advent of offering delivery and pickup service for simple alcoholic beverages and appetizers. All bars and lounges will soon offer this service if they want to stay in tune with the competition, as this trend doesn't seem to have a downside for any bars, and the convenience is too good to pass up for patrons.

The World Changes

Modern updates not only consists of keeping up with the latest food crazes and technologies, but also the latest changes in the economy and the world; as the world changes, as people change, as the economy changes, restaurateurs must follow the trends in order to stay afloat; there are no easy updates, but if the time is taken to modernize and develop new and innovative ways to offer service, a restaurant will have the longevity necessary to remain relevant.

CHAPTER 5: EMPLOYEE RETENTION

Hire The Right People From The Start

Hiring the right people from the moment they apply to the position can be easier said than done, but it can be done. Here's a list of different actions you can take to ensure you're hiring the right employee for the job:

❖ When you solicit for the position you are attempting to fill, make sure you are very precise about the position you need filled. Potential employees need to know exactly what would be expected of them if they decide to work for your establishment. Be clear about their everyday tasks, hours needed, position within the company, and salary (yes I said salary); job seekers are more enthusiastic about a position if they know what they are getting into financially; they need reassurance that their expenses will be covered working for your establishment.

❖ Make sure to mention your corporate culture, and your company philosophies, so your potential employee understands your mindset before attempting to work for an establishment they may not necessarily fit into.

❖ When listing the position available, make sure to list all required experience so that the potential employee has a clear understanding of what they are expected to know before applying. The job seeker must also be confident when applying to the position, and knowing that their background matches perfectly to what their potential employer is looking for in an employee, motivates the best candidates to apply.

❖ Once you receive a resume, take your time and look through them thoroughly. Go through each resume with a fine-toothed comb, from work experience to education, then come up with a list of candidates that fit your idea of the best people for the position. Make sure to concentrate more on experience than anything else, even education; education will only teach someone so much, but experience goes a longer way when hiring someone for a brand-new position, that may not have immediate training. It is important to note, someone who is educated in a specific field should be given a chance as well, but experience trumps education; the best way to determine the best fit in this situation is to interview both types of candidates and see what they have to offer.

❖ The Call: A really good way to decrease your potential employee resume pile is to make the initial call to setup an interview with the candidate. A lot of times you may get resumes from people that aren't really that interested in working, but filled out your application anyway just to have something to show to unemployment or an interested party; you will weed out those duds as soon as you make your call to setup an interview; either the candidate won't answer the call, will hang up once they realize it's you, or will pretend they're not quite sure what date would work for them to interview, and they'll say they will get back to you, and you will never hear from them again.

When I worked for a finance company I got a lot of resumes from people that really had no intention of coming in for an interview, and I would leave a message on their voicemail, wait twenty-four hours for a return phone call, and if I didn't hear from them, I would then throw away the resume and move on to the next candidate; my pile was consistently low.

❖ Ask the right questions: Your candidate got through all of the stops, and now they're sitting in front of you and you're ready to get to the most important part of the process for both employer and employee, the interview. You must ask the questions you want answers to, as long as the questions don't violate the law. Sitting down and writing out all of the questions that you know are pertinent to the position, is essential before any interview. You must not take this portion of the process lightly and just come up with questions on the fly, you must be prepared. Every question must target, not only the job candidate's mindset when it comes to the position, but also the candidate's enthusiasm about the position, and their overall understanding of your restaurant, and where you would like it to be in the projected future, and if that candidate thinks of themselves as going along with you and your business for the ride. Assessing this dire information will help in ensuring a long-lasting, on-going, healthy relationship between restaurateur and employees.

Employee Assessments

Employee assessments are essential to any business, and I'm sure every entrepreneur understands this fact, but why assessments are important may differ from entrepreneur to entrepreneur. Owners, managers, supervisors should understand that the employee assessments should only be to assess the employee's understanding of their position, and their future potential with the company pertaining to their position, and maybe a future promotion; employee assessments should not be used to try and fire an employee, but to assess their ability to do their job properly, then make the necessary adjustments needed to either provide more training if needed, give the employee a raise for their good work, or promote the employee in order to keep them working for you as a long-term asset to your restaurant. This type of assessment gives your employee a sense of stability knowing that they will be evaluated fairly and given a chance to gain knowledge of their position and/or increase their responsibilities, allowing them to feel appreciated guaranteeing their long-term service.

Patrons Get To Know Your Employees

It can be difficult for restaurateurs to get to know their employees, especially if running multiple locations with hundreds or even thousands of employees, so a lot of times employees can be just a face or a name, with no real personality to attach to that face or name, but just because an employer doesn't know their employee on an intricate level, doesn't mean their patrons don't know them in that way. Many times, patrons get to know employees on a personal level, that even employees don't realize until they're told. If employers only pay attention to the word of a manager, supervisor, or even one complaint by a customer, they may be missing out on the bigger asset that the employee has to offer; it may be that the employee provides a service to your regular patrons that may be valuable enough for them to keep coming back. Take into consideration your patron/employee relationships before you make any rash decisions to let go of any of your workers, including those employees that seem expendable to their coworkers.

CHAPTER 6: CUSTOMER APPRECIATION

They Deserve Your Appreciation

Thank You

A thank you can go a long way in making a patron smile. As a patron of a restaurant, I'm sure you've encountered those times when the manager or owner of a restaurant came explicitly to your table and thanked you for choosing to dine at their specific establishment; the owner's appreciation made your dining experience that much more special, and I'm sure sealed the deal for you to navigate back to their restaurant the next time you get a hankering for the food they offer, as opposed to the competition. Verbally thanking patrons is quick, easy, painless, and satisfying, and yet so many restaurateurs forget this small but powerful marketing tool.

Discounts

Every restaurateur should know their best customers. A great way to keep track of them is through a subscriber list; collecting patron's emails is not just considered something that informal fast-food restaurants do anymore, it is now accepted in formal spaces as well. It used to be considered unprofessional or in bad taste to offer discounts for formal dining, but now formal restaurants have picked up on this trend and now offer discounts to their frequent patrons, along with emailed coupons and deals for the next visit. Offering these perks to your regular patrons makes them feel special and acknowledged, while it helps you keep track of your consistent customers and helps lure them back into your establishment for more pampering.

Customer Appreciation Day

Why not have a customer appreciation day? This is a day for not only your customers to be shown your appreciation for their frequenting of your establishment, but it's also a day for your staff to be acknowledged for their hard work in providing the best service to your best customers. Customer appreciation day allows everyone, including the restaurateur, to get to know each other on a more personal level, as you all celebrate the hard work and dedication everyone has put into giving the special attention it takes to keep your customers happy, while your customers enjoy your best offerings at a tremendous discount or even free. Customer appreciation day should be an annual event during the week, and should be attended by all staff, with invites for all of your subscribed patrons, sent at least three months in advance, with reminders every few weeks, then days, then hours, before the big event; many will attend and all will remember to come back to your restaurant because of your appreciation for their patronage.

CHAPTER 7: LISTEN

Hear Your Customers

Your Employees Hear It All

So many employers will hire employees to work for them but don't trust a word they say about anything, even when it comes to customer satisfaction. It is a shame that this happens so often, but it does, which inevitably causes many establishments to shut down due to the owner not really knowing what their customers wanted or needed from them. Restaurateurs must listen to their employees when it comes to their assessment of the patrons and what it is that they are seeking from their establishment. Employees have a much better position to really hear what the patrons are saying, either to the employee themselves or to each other. It is important to believe your staff, trust their judgment and make changes accordingly, so that everyone feels empowered to contribute to the success of the restaurant.

Your Customers Don't Lie

Think about it, how often does someone go into a restaurant just to sabotage the restaurant and give it a bad name by reviewing it in a nasty terrible way? Most of the time diners are just going to a restaurant to have a great meal, great time with their loved ones, and a relaxing night out, enjoying food that they didn't have to prepare that day; most patrons are not out to get the restaurant owner by bad mouthing them in order to put them out of business, and yet restaurateurs have a hard time believing patrons when they have a complaint. It is not the patron; it is your restaurant that needs help. I know it's hard to believe, but if a patron complains about food service, food, atmosphere, ambiance, staff, any part of your establishment, you should be looking into what they are complaining about, and taking it very seriously. No one should take a complaint lightly, but especially not restaurateurs, because that can spell disaster in your case, one bad review can shut down your establishment.

I once read a review about a popular buffet chain that I used to frequent quite often and the woman mentioned that there was a roach on the desserts; at first I didn't really think it was true, but then she began to describe how she told management about this roach, and the manager shrugged it off, walked over to the roach, wiped it off the desserts and walked away stating that it was no big deal; needless to say, I never went back.

Listen to your patrons and if they look and sound very concerned, you should too. Don't take what they say gently and don't make it seem like their complaint is no big deal; you may not ever have a situation like the above scenario (hopefully not), but every patron's comments, suggestions, and concerns are important, truthful, and should be taken seriously; whether from the mouth of the patron themselves, or from your employees, all matters must be heard, listened to, and addressed in a timely fashion. If you hear your employees and patrons, you will retain them no matter the situation.

CHAPTER 8: RETAINING YOUR CUSTOMERS:

IT'S THAT EASY

Let Us Help You

These are the 7 basic steps to retaining your restaurant diners; there is so much detail that goes into each step. Coello Critiques, provides our own personalized restaurant critiques, for your convenience, so that you don't have to face the critics unprepared. We will critique your establishment(s) before they do; Atmosphere, service, decor, inclusion access, kid friendliness, and our own Double C Star Rating system; we review, analyze, and describe your restaurant specifics in a private comprehensive report so that you can guide and prepare your staff for 2020 and beyond. We also reward each of our clients with our Coello Critique's plaque with your Double C Star Rating of 2.0 or more, to set the stage for your success.

Book your private comprehensive review with Coello Critiques. You will find multiple packages available for your specific needs. Type in the address below into your URL and book with us today!

Type into your url:
https://www.coellocritiques.com

ABOUT THE AUTHOR

Shirley Coello has been writing since the young age of eight years old, when her mother used to have her and her siblings write for the Pennysaver contests she saw in the paper, as an extracurricular activity. Shirley's specialty was writing horror stories with a twist, even though she was afraid of them and hated watching any type of horror flicks on television.

Many books and horror stories later, Shirley embarked on working in the world of customer service, manufacturing, healthcare, finance, insurance, and hospitality throughout her working career; in addition to working as a content writer for a handful of dot commers.

After over thirty years of working experience, Shirley has combined her love for writing and her work experience to bring you a series of books in the works, sharing her expertise learned through experience and a business degree specializing in Business Administration. The point of these business books is to lend some insight into how businesses are run and how they could be run better, not just for the business owner, but for the employees as well. Shirley knows firsthand what it is like to work in operations, mid-level management, and upper management, and provides a clear-cut detailed synopsis of business and how to thrive within the chaos of it all.

Reading Shirley's books will give entrepreneurs a sense of relief as they try to navigate through the hectic world of business, industry, and paperwork. Shirley gives a step by step informative so that everyone reading, upper, mid, or lower management, and/or operations can not only understand their role in the business, but have a sense of empathy for those outside of their own positions, in order for the work place as a whole to be the best it could be for any industry.

ABOUT COELLO CRITIQUES

Coello Critiques was created for the restaurateur and their patrons with a mindset of preparing restaurant owners for the inevitable review from their customers. Working in the catering industry from the age of ten years old, I understand how much work and energy goes into the perfect preparation for guests, and being a restaurant frequenter, I also understand the other side of hospitality and what patrons expect from the restaurateur.

Coello Critiques began solely as an interesting project for the Coello family to embark on; a journey of sorts, to put our restaurant hopping to work. Our family loves to eat out and we love fine dining, although at one point it was few and far in between, we still loved to watch cooking shows that would highlight the fine dining experience, and we would dream of one day enhancing our portfolio of fine dining to surpass our one trip to The London in Manhattan New York, when the girls were only 3 and 2 years old, and our boy was just in the womb.

As the children grew and finances dwindled eating out at any restaurant became a luxury that we just could not afford, but we bit the bullet and did it anyway, determined to give our children a sense of sophisticated experience, even if only from the table of a fine restaurant like Carrabba's. The children learned at a very young age how to present themselves while dining at a restaurant, and always had the spotlight as restaurant staff noticed their proper behavior, the way in which they ordered their appetizers, main course, and desserts, politely, and their disciplined eating habits, while they admired the restaurant aesthetic. Needless to say, my children love the public dining experience, and since they have experienced it since they were laying in their car-seats, they have a unique perspective of each and every restaurant, from food to ambiance, from service to menu, from location to demographic; my children have the expertise of a seasoned restaurant lover as I and my husband do.

The decision to turn this love of dining from a hobby to a full-time job came with ease, as I set out to provide customer service training for all industries; I began to think of ways to teach proper customer service to restaurants, when I realized that there was so much more to professionalism than just how customers are greeted or even served in a restaurant; Restaurateurs needed to really get a picture of their establishment as a whole, and I knew that we were the perfect family to give them just that, a picture of the overall workings of their business, and how it effects all families; we were going to be the eyes, ears, and mouth for all, without the public criticism that can come with reviews; we could actually help the restaurateur fix the issues and gain more customers, all with just our observation: Coello Critiques was born.

Coello Critiques offers a unique side of reviewing because we offer perspectives from many different age groups, genres, and sexes in order to provide the best overall review of your establishment, coming from the mindset of an entire family dynamic, demographic, and cultural experience. We embody the perspective of the average American family, and not just one individual person of a distinct age, culture, genre, sex, etc., we encompass your entire target patron. Our unique cultural backgrounds also allow for an appreciation of multiple tastes, flavors, and pallets. Throughout the years just experimenting with our own different cultural cuisine distinctions has educated us in how wonderful a variation of cultural flavors can be, and how to appreciate all culture's cuisines and the traditions that they are made from.

Hiring Coello Critiques is the only way the restaurateur will be able to get a fresh perspective of their establishment from an entire family that will truly give a detailed report and perspective, before they make the plunge to open their doors to the public, without having flaws publicized for the world to see. We critique you before they do.

DOUBLE C STAR RATING (Food)

Food Rating System

Coello Critique's version of the Michelin Star, the Double C Star Rating: Food Section, is the food rating system of Coello Critiques. Coello critiques will focus on your restaurant cuisine as a separate scoring system from the ambiance and service rating.

Our Cuisine Scoring System:

- ✓ Written Appeal – Is the name of the meal appealing?

- ✓ Sight – Does the cuisine look appealing? We first eat with our eyes.

- ✓ Presentation – Is the food served on an appropriate surface (plate, skillet, bowl, etc.)

- ✓ Taste – How does the food taste?

- ✓ Financial Appeal – Is the cuisine worth the amount of money spent on the meal?

- ✓ Food Regulations – Does the food meet all state/federal regulatory requirements (stated potential allergic reaction to seasonings, etc.)

✓ Ingredients – Does the ingredients of the cuisine fit the standard ingredient list for the dish and/or add/subtract flavor profiles?

✓ Overall Cuisine Experience – All together, did the dish meet expectations?

The above questions are considered and based on the cuisine experience, given 1 to 3 stars. We then take the average of those stars to arrive at our Double C Star Rating.

www.ingramcontent.com/pod-product-compliance
Lightning Source LLC
Chambersburg PA
CBHW030543220526
45463CB00007B/2957